HEALTHY EATING

Nancy Dickmann

Published by Brown Bear Books Ltd
4877 N. Circulo Bujia
Tucson, AZ 85718
USA

and

G14, Regent Studios
1 Thane Villas
London N7 7PH
UK

© 2025 Brown Bear Books Ltd

ISBN 978-1-83572-005-9 (ALB)
ISBN 978-1-83572-011-0 (paperback)
ISBN 978-1-83572-017-2 (ebook)

All rights reserved. No part of this book may be reproduced, stored in a retrieval system, or transmitted, in any form or by any means, electronic, mechanical, photocopying, recording, or otherwise, without the prior written permission of the copyright holder.

Library of Congress Cataloging-in-Publication Data available on request

Designer: Trudi Webb
Design Manager: Keith Davis
Children's Publisher: Anne O'Daly
Picture Manager: Sophie Mortimer

Picture Credits
Cover: Shutterstock: Blueastro, Your Universe and Shutterstock Vector Stock Library.
Interior: Shutterstock: ann131313 6, Anna.zabella 11, brgfx 12, Ailey Daily 9, IGOR Deyka 8, GoodStudio 19, Iconic Bestiary 14, mentalmind 13, PCH Vector 16, Andrew Rybalko 4, Sabel Skaya 17, StockSmartStudio 15, 18, Tarikdiz 10, Tartila 5, 21, Tenstudio 1, Topconcept 20, Vita_Dor 7.

All other artwork, Brown Bear Books and Shutterstock Vector Stock Library.

Brown Bear Books has made every attempt to contact the copyright holder.
If you have any information about omissions, please contact: licensing@brownbearbooks.co.uk

Manufactured in the United States of America
CPSIA compliance information: Batch#AG/5662

Websites
The website addresses in this book were valid at the time of going to press. However, it is possible that contents or addresses may change following publication of this book. No responsibility for any such changes can be accepted by the author or the publisher. Readers should be supervised when they access the Internet.

Contents

Fuel Your Body! 4

Nutrients 6

Plant Power 8

Meat and Dairy 10

Grains 12

Fats, Sugar, and Salt 14

Water 16

How Much? 18

A Balanced Diet 20

Your Turn! 22

Find Out More 22

Glossary 23

Index 24

Fuel Your Body!

Machines need fuel to run. Your body needs fuel, too!

We power computers and lights with electricity. We fill some cars with gas. Others plug in to charge up. Even an old-fashioned windmill needs wind power to move.

Your body is no different. It needs fuel too. That fuel is the food you eat.

A bicycle needs power to move. The power comes from your muscles.

It can be hard to tell which foods are the healthiest.

Making Choices

All machines need the right fuel to work properly. There are many foods to choose from. Some are healthier than others. Which ones will you choose? Healthy foods are the best way to power your body. They'll keep you happy and healthy. They'll give you lots of energy!

The average person spends a little over **one hour** eating each day. That's nearly **16** days a year!

1 hour

16 days

Nutrients

Food contains materials that your body can use.

Nutrients are substances in food. They help you live and grow. Your digestive system breaks down the food you eat. Your body takes in the nutrients. They are sent where they need to go. Each nutrient has a different job. Some give you energy. Others build strong bones.

Big and Small
We only need small amounts of vitamins and minerals.

We need bigger amounts of fats, proteins, and carbohydrates.

Oranges contain vitamin C. This nutrient helps you fight off illness.

Kinds of Nutrients

There are lots of different nutrients.
They all fit into one of seven main types.

1. Carbohydrates give you energy.
2. Proteins help muscles grow strong.
3. Fats give you energy.
   They help your body take in vitamins.
4. Minerals come from the earth.
   They keep your body running smoothly.
5. Vitamins come from plants or animals.
   They help your body work well.
6. Fiber helps keep your gut healthy.
7. Water helps carry nutrients around the body.
   It gets rid of wastes.

Try to eat a wide range of different foods.
That way you'll get all the nutrients you need!

Plant Power

Plants are important for a healthy diet. We eat lots of different kinds.

We eat different parts of plants. Apples and grapes are fruits. Fruits protect a plant's seeds. Vegetables are other parts of a plant. Carrots are roots. Celery is a stem. We eat many fruits and vegetables raw. They can also be cooked. Some are made into juice.

Many fruits and vegetables go bad quickly. Canning makes them last longer.

The fresher the fruit or veg, the healthier it is. Freezing helps fruit and veg keep their nutrients.

Eat a Rainbow!

Fruits and vegetables contain carbohydrates. They give you energy. These foods are also full of fiber. Each one has a mix of different vitamins and minerals. Sweet potatoes are rich in vitamin A. Broccoli has a lot of iron. Try to eat fruits and vegetables in different colors. You'll get a good range of vitamins and minerals.

Which of these vegetables is a stem?

A. green bean

B. spinach

C. celery

Meat and Dairy

Some food comes from animals. It has lots of protein.

Your muscles are mainly made of protein. So are the muscles of animals. That makes meat a good source of protein. Eggs and milk come from animals, too. Milk can be made into cheese, yogurt, or ice cream. These foods are all rich in protein.

Fish has a lot of protein. Salmon also has oils that help your brain.

Nuts and seeds are a quick, healthy snack. You can also add them to salads or pasta.

Protein from Plants

Vegetarians don't eat meat. They get their protein from plants! Beans, peas, and lentils are packed with protein. They also have plenty of fiber. Tofu and soya milk are made from soybeans. That's another good protein source. There is protein in nuts and seeds as well.

Meat Swaps
There are foods that we can eat instead of meat. They're made from fungus. They have lots of protein. You can swap them for ground beef or pork.

Grains

We often eat plants called cereal grasses. Their seeds and fruits are called grains.

Most people eat grains every day. Wheat and oats are grains. Rice and barley are grains, too. Grains are a good source of carbohydrates. Wheat is often ground into flour. It's used to make other foods. Bread and pasta are usually made from wheat flour.

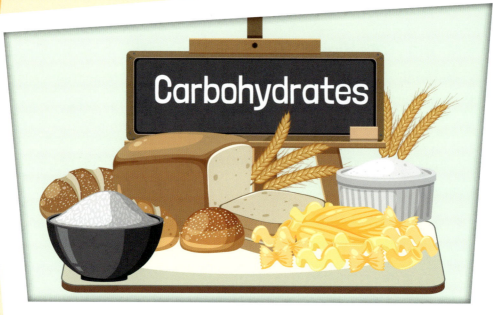

Grains are carbohydrates.
Which of your favorite foods are made from grains?

Whole Grains

Each tiny kernel of grain has a shell. The shell is rich in fiber, iron, and vitamins. Often when grains are ground into flour, this shell is removed. This takes away some of the nutrients. Wholegrain foods keep the shell. They are much healthier. Try to choose wholegrain bread, pasta, and cereals.

Check the label on your bread. Is it made from whole grains?

About **half** the grains we eat should be whole grains. But most people only eat about **15%**.

Fats, Sugar, and Salt

Many foods contain fats, sugar, and salt. They are less healthy.

Do you like french fries and ice cream? How about cola and chocolate? These foods have some nutrients, such as carbohydrates. But they also have lots of sugar, fat, and salt. Eating too much of these foods is bad for you. Save them for occasional treats.

Many people think salty, sugary, or fatty foods taste good. That's why we eat them!

Frying food adds a lot of fat. Choose foods that are baked or steamed instead.

Added to Food

We often use fats when we cook. Some fats are healthier than others. Olive oil and vegetable oil are a better choice than butter. Packaged foods like cereal, sauces, and cookies often have added sugar or salt. Always check the labels. That way you'll know what you're eating!

Which of these foods are high in salt?
A. potato chips
B. cheese
C. bacon
D. all of the above

Water

What do you drink? It's just as important as what you eat!

Water doesn't have fats or protein. It doesn't have vitamins. But it's still a key part of your diet! Your body is about 60% water. You lose water when you sweat, breathe, or pee. Drinking replaces the water you lose. You also get water from the foods you eat.

Watermelon tastes really juicy. That's because it's mostly water!

Staying Hydrated

Drinking water keeps you hydrated. This means your body has enough water to work properly. Juice, soda, or sports drinks keep you hydrated. But they usually have a lot of sugar. Water or milk are the best choices! Milk has protein. It also has calcium to help your bones and teeth.

When you're active, you sweat more. Make sure to keep drinking water!

Try to drink **6 to 8** glasses of water each day. You'll need more if it's hot!

How Much?

Choosing healthy foods is important. But how much should you eat?

The energy in food is measured in calories. Your body burns calories as you breathe, move, and grow. You need to eat enough food to replace the calories you burn. If you eat more than you need, your body stores the extra as fat. Getting the balance right helps you stay at a healthy weight.

Running uses up more calories than sitting on the sofa.

Everyone has different calorie needs. Your parents might have bigger bodies. But you might be more active.

Snacks

People often snack between meals. Snacks can give you an energy boost. They might keep you from eating too much later. But it's best to keep snacks healthy and small.

Portion Sizes

There's no easy answer to how much food you need. It depends on your age and your size. It also depends on how active you are. Children usually need less food than adults. Try to only eat when you're hungry. Stop when you feel full, even if there's food left on your plate.

19

A Balanced Diet

What's the key to a healthy diet?
It's all about balance.

Different foods have different nutrients. To get all the nutrients you need, eat a good mix of healthy foods each day. You need fruits and vegetables. You also need grains and protein foods. Vegetables and grains should be the biggest groups on your plate.

Try to eat five servings of fruit or vegetables every day.

Planning Meals

Think about what you put on your plate. What ingredients are in each dish? Veggie chili has vegetables as well as protein-rich beans. Add a whole grain, such as brown rice. A piece of fruit makes a good side dish. Add a cup of yogurt for dessert for extra protein. That's a balanced meal!

> **Which of these dishes contains four different food groups?**
>
> A. pasta with tomato sauce and cheese
>
> B. pizza topped with ham and pineapple
>
> C. hamburger on a bun with lettuce

Making healthy meals is something the whole family can enjoy!

Your Turn!

You can take responsibility for healthy eating! Here are some ideas.

1. Keep a food diary for a few weeks. Write down what you eat. Then look back to see what you could improve. Are you eating a good range of the different food groups?

2. Help your grown-up plan a week of balanced meals. Look for chances to add healthier options. You could swap wholegrain bread for white bread. Work together to make a shopping list.

Find Out More

Books

Koster, Gloria. *Vegetables Are Good for You! (Healthy Foods)*. Mankato, Minn.: Capstone Press, 2023.

Olson, Elsie. *Be Well!: A Hero's Guide to a Healthy Mind and Body (Be Your Best You!)*. Minneapolis, Minn.: Super Sandcastle, 2020.

Woolley, Katie. *Eating Well (My Healthy Life)*. New York: Rosen Publishing, 2024.

Websites

kids.britannica.com/kids/article/food-and-nutrition/353140

kidshealth.org/en/kids/go-slow-whoa.html

www.myplate.gov/life-stages/kids

Glossary

calcium a mineral that the body uses to build healthy bones and teeth

calorie a unit for measuring the amount of energy that a food contains

carbohydrate a chemical substance, such as a sugar, made by plants; the human body uses carbohydrates to produce and store energy

digestive system the parts of the body, such as the stomach and intestines, that break down food so that the body can use its nutrients

energy the power or ability to work or be active; we use energy when we move and grow

fat an oily substance found in plants or animals, which the human body can use as a source of energy

fungus a member of the group of plant-like living things that includes mushrooms

grains the small hard seeds of cereal plants such as wheat or rice; grains are often ground into flour

mineral a substance formed in the earth, such as calcium or potassium, that the body needs in small amounts to stay healthy

nutrient a substance in food that people, plants, or animals can use to grow and survive

protein a type of nutrient found in all living things, which the human body uses to build muscle and other tissues

vegetarian a person who chooses not to eat meat

vitamin a chemical substance found in food that helps the body work properly

Index

A
animals 7, 10

B
body 4, 5, 6, 7, 16, 17, 18
bones 6, 17
brain 10
bread 12, 13

C
calories 18, 19
carbohydrates 6, 7, 9, 12, 14
cooking 8, 15

E
energy 5, 6, 7, 9, 18

F
fats 6, 7, 14, 15, 16
fiber 7, 9, 11, 13

flour 12, 13
food labels 13, 15
fruits 8, 9, 12, 20, 21
frying 15
fuel 4, 5

G
grains 12, 13, 20
growing 6, 7, 18

H
healthy foods 5, 13, 15, 18, 20

M
meat 10, 11
minerals 6, 7, 9
muscles 4, 7, 10

N
nutrients 6, 7, 9, 13, 14, 20

P
pasta 11, 12, 13
plants 7, 8, 9, 11, 12
protein 6, 7, 10, 11, 16, 17, 20, 21

S
salt 14, 15
seeds 8, 11, 12
snacks 11, 19
sugar 14, 15, 17
sweating 16, 17

V
vegetables 8, 9, 20, 21
vitamins 6, 7, 9, 13, 16

W
water 7, 16, 17
whole grains 13, 21

Answers to Questions

page 9: C (celery is a stem, while a green bean is a seed pod and spinach is a leaf)

page 15: D (potato chips, cheese, and bacon all contain high amounts of salt, so you should only eat them in small amounts)

page 21: B Hawaiian pizza (grains in the crust, fruit in the tomato sauce and the pineapple, dairy in the cheese, meat as ham). The pasta and hamburger have only three food groups each.